STYLE YOUR *MIND*

FOR SUCCESS

MINDSET MASTERY FOR THE
CONFIDENCE AND CLARITY TO
TRANSFORM YOUR BUSINESS

CARA ALWILL LEYBA

AUTHOR OF *GIRL CODE*

Style Your Mind *For Success*

For more, visit www.CaraAlwill.com
or email Info@CaraAlwill.com

INTRODUCTION

What if you decided you were no longer available for average?

Imagine waking up every day, feeling absolutely certain that you are about to do your best work. Imagine being so obsessed with your own life, that the idea of comparing yourself to a stranger on social media seems laughable. Envision yourself, completely aligned with the woman you know you're meant to be: thinking like her, dressing like her, doing business like her, earning income like her, attracting dream opportunities like her. Imagine reclaiming your time, *owning* your day, and truly, finally, stepping into your power as a successful business woman.

I can vividly recall fantasizing about the life I have right now. Just a few short years ago, sitting under the fluorescent-lit cubicle at my day job, I desperately dreamed of walking into The Plaza Hotel, placing my jumbo black caviar leather Chanel purse on the seat next to me, and ordering a lobster salad and a glass of Veuve Clicquot. In my mind, I would open my brand new rose gold Mac air book, log into my email, and read countless emails from women whose lives I had touched. While sipping my crisp, ice-cold glass of bubbly, I'd sign on new coaching clients, field emails from my book editor, and make plans for that evening to try that hot new restaurant that had just opened. Some days I'd fantasize about flying first-class from New York to London to meet with my U.K. publisher to go do press for my new book. Some days I'd imagine spending an entire afternoon in my fluffy, white bath robe, simply deciding that the day would be better spent leisurely relaxing in bed, because that's what I craved energetically.

I get chills as I write all of this, because *every single thing* in that visualization came true. And it continues to come true. **This is my new standard of living**.

But that wasn't always my story. Raised by a single mother and left by a drug-addicted, deadbeat father, I didn't grow up with money, mentors, or anyone to open a door for me. I knew from a young age I'd need to create my own opportunities. Although I didn't have much, I had dreams, and those were my most valuable asset. My passion drove me. I knew I wanted a better life for myself, and I knew the path to get there would require a laser-focused belief in myself.

But it took time. And faith. And confidence. And waking up every morning going to a job I hated because I had to pay the bills. And trying new things, and failing, and trying again. And sneaking into Facebook groups when my co-workers weren't looking, and asking millions of questions to other women entrepreneurs who were 10 steps ahead of me. And facing rejection after rejection. And spending my last dollars to pay for coaching courses because I knew the power of personal development if I was ever going to get the hell out of that reality and create a new one. And using my own knowledge as a life coach to work through my own bullshit and master my own mind.

Here's the thing: I always knew, deep down, that I was meant for more. I knew I had great business ideas. I knew how to write blogs and post on social media. I knew how to life coach. And what I didn't know, I could hire someone to do. So why wasn't I fully embodying everything I wanted in my life? Why couldn't I pull the trigger on my dreams and live without fear? Why couldn't I fully *be* the woman I wanted to be?

It wasn't another webinar on marketing strategies that I needed. **I needed a way to eradicate those dream-slaughtering beliefs that continually crept into the back of my mind.** Those scary "adult" voices of parents and accountants warning against *fantasy worlds* and urging me to cling to any old boring job simply because it offered a retirement plan. I had to get over the fear of hearing the "Who does she think she is?" voice from every mean girl I'd ever met. And I had to learn to overcome the biggest bully of all - myself.

Through my extensive training and education as a life coach, my immersion in the positive psychology and optimal living world, and my experience and success as a personal development author, I was able to completely transform my own life. I was able to muster the courage to walk away from my day job, with little to no savings, and take a chance on myself. I created and implemented my own powerful mindset shifts, custom strategies, and actionable steps to raise my vibration and program my mind for success.

I am now a bestselling author of seven personal development books, the host of a top-rated podcast with 4 million listeners in just a little over a year, a high-earning life coach with clients around the world, and a woman who is so incredibly fulfilled and excited about every single day (and I am no longer under those fluorescent lights!).

I have gone on to help thousands of other women transform their lives and businesses. And now I want to help you.

It may be leaving your day job. It may be getting to the next level in your business. It may be ascending to the most exquisite version of yourself so that you can show up in the world and finally do what you are meant to do. It may be upgrading your life and deciding you are no longer available for struggle. You decide what success looks like for you. Together, we'll work through my proven processes and style your mind to make it all happen.

WHY I CREATED THIS

After spending a decade in the self-help space, both personally and professionally, I noticed one resounding theme: lots of very excited, passionate women losing their zest for entrepreneurship just as quickly as they found it.

Year after year, I'd meet new business women at networking events, in my social circles, through coaching masterminds and on social media who were frustrated. They'd invested thousands of dollars with business coaches and self-proclaimed "gurus" who promised blueprints to success. They were overdosing on webinars, books, and very expensive seminars hoping to find a one-size-fits-all approach to business. And none of it was working long-term, nor did it feel natural or authentic to them, because there is no one-size-fits-all blueprint for success. They were overwhelmed and uninspired, and losing hope fast.

These women knew the importance of nurturing their business, but they were missing one incredibly important piece of the puzzle: _mastering their own mindset_.

And I'm not just talking about reading *The Secret* or listening to a podcast about affirmations. The work required to build a solid understanding of yourself in the role of an entrepreneur is intense. And without a solid understanding of who you are in this brave new world of business, you'll find it nearly impossible to overcome the inevitable challenges, grit through difficult times, make confident decisions, and achieve long-term success. This kind of mastery takes dedication to self-awareness and the tools to practice it daily. It takes the guidance and mentoring from a professional woman who has been there herself, and helped thousands of other women through it as well.

You may have read my bestselling book *Girl Code*. In it, I share my own personal experiences in building my business, along with interviews with other female entrepreneurs from all different industries about how they built theirs. Filled with inspirational stories and mindset shifts, *Girl Code* has become a global sensation. But as successful as the book has been, I knew my audience craved more. You wanted a deeper dive, including actionable, practical tools to help you take that inspiration and create real change in your lives.

I created *Style Your Mind For Success* for female entrepreneurs who want to increase their energetic vibration, build their confidence, get crystal clear on their vision, and become success magnets. As a certified master life coach and bestselling personal development author, I know one thing to be true: Your business will only thrive if you do.

I have worked with countless women through my books, courses, and private coaching programs over the years to help them elevate their thoughts, upgrade their standards, and renew their sense of self. My clients have shifted from feeling low-energy, overwhelmed, and confused, to feeling razor-sharp, aligned, and filled with joy for their lives and businesses. They have grown the same way I have. They continue to level up the same way I do, every day.

I am obsessed with helping women transform their businesses by elevating their thoughts and upgrading their lives. Consider *Style Your Mind For Success* an opportunity for me to be your private business coach. Are you ready?

THIS IS FOR YOU IF:

You're still not experiencing the success you desire in your business

You spend a lot of time in your head

You don't *feel* successful

You compare yourself to everyone else in your industry

You're afraid to ask for sales and you aren't making the money you want to make

You desperately want to live your passion, feel in flow, and do what you love with certainty

You feel unorganized and overwhelmed in your life and business

You don't really know who you are as a business woman (you find yourself trying to emulate other women's business style)

Your inner circle doesn't really "get" what you do (most people think you play on Facebook all day or your side hustle is a hobby)

You often feel guilty for putting yourself first

You don't feel as powerful as you know you could

THROUGH THIS EXPERIENCE, I WILL TEACH YOU TO:

Get crystal clear on your vision for your business

Understand the power of confidence and show you how to cultivate it in every moment

Create an energetic outline for your life so that you can serve yourself and your clients better

Decide the woman you want to be and embody her fully

Curate your circle both online and offline so that you are completely supported

Redefine success on your own terms

Get over your fear of failure and realize the value in certain things not working out

Establish and implement success rituals and powerful ways of living every day

Sound good? Before we begin, you'll need to trash any beliefs that you cannot design the business and the life of your dreams. The only way to make the most of this experience is to believe that everything is possible. I'll be asking you some tough questions - it's on you to answer them truthfully. It's time to get real with yourself, push your own limits, and finally understand that you deserve it all.

Let's do this.

CONTENTS

SET YOUR INTENTION

Why did you pick up this workbook?

_____

_____

_____

_____

_____

_____

_____

_____

_____

_____

_____

_____

_____

_____

_____

_____

_____

What do you hope to gain from this experience?

_____

_____

_____

_____

_____

_____

_____

_____

_____

_____

_____

_____

_____

_____

_____

_____

_____

_____

How can you make the most of this?

_____

_____

_____

_____

_____

_____

_____

_____

_____

_____

_____

_____

_____

_____

_____

_____

_____

What will success look like for you at the end of this experience?

_____

_____

_____

_____

_____

_____

_____

_____

_____

_____

_____

_____

_____

_____

_____

_____

_____

WHAT'S A VIBE GOT TO DO WITH IT?

The first step to making any real change in our lives and our businesses is to change our energy. Our energy, or vibration, is the frequency we put out into the world that determines the quality of our experiences. When we are in a high vibration, we choose positive, optimistic thoughts, which ultimately create a positive, optimistic reality for us.

For example, if you're constantly stressed about not making enough money in your business, you're likely in a low vibration. Anxiety, stress, negative self-talk, and fear are all examples of feelings that create a low vibration. And when you're in a low vibration, you're focusing on everything you *don't* have, which blocks you from being able to find solutions.

On the other hand, if you're in creative flow, and focusing on creating new programs or products, you're likely in a high vibration. Optimism, creativity, gratitude, and joy are all examples of feelings that create a high vibration. Being in a high vibration brings forth new ideas, attracts your dream clients, makes you more money, and catapults your success.

Getting in a high vibe is the quickest way to supercharge your soul and skyrocket your success. Remember: You have the power to redirect your thoughts at any time. So how do you get there? Here are a few questions to help you shift into a high vibration in your business:

QUESTIONS TO EMPOWER YOUR BUSINESS

How do you want to feel as a woman?

_____

_____

_____

_____

_____

_____

_____

_____

_____

_____

_____

_____

_____

_____

_____

_____

_____

How do you want your business to feel?

_____

_____

_____

_____

_____

_____

_____

_____

_____

_____

_____

_____

_____

_____

_____

_____

_____

_____

_____

What would you love to happen in your business right now?

_____

_____

_____

_____

_____

_____

_____

_____

_____

_____

_____

_____

_____

_____

_____

_____

_____

What tasks in your business give you energy?

_____

_____

_____

_____

_____

_____

_____

_____

_____

_____

_____

_____

_____

_____

_____

_____

_____

What tasks in your business drain you?

_____

_____

_____

_____

_____

_____

_____

_____

_____

_____

_____

_____

_____

_____

_____

_____

_____

How can you eliminate or delegate those tasks?

_____

_____

_____

_____

_____

_____

_____

_____

_____

_____

_____

_____

_____

_____

_____

_____

_____

_____

_____

How can you create your most incredible day?

_____

_____

_____

_____

_____

_____

_____

_____

_____

_____

_____

_____

_____

_____

_____

_____

_____

_____

_____

What type of clients excite you?

_____

_____

_____

_____

_____

_____

_____

_____

_____

_____

_____

_____

_____

_____

_____

_____

_____

_____

_____

_____

What type of clients drain you?

_____

_____

_____

_____

_____

_____

_____

_____

_____

_____

_____

_____

_____

_____

_____

_____

_____

_____

How can you ensure you only work with clients that give you energy?

_____

_____

_____

_____

_____

_____

_____

_____

_____

_____

_____

_____

_____

_____

_____

_____

_____

Think about a time you were in a high vibration. What did it feel like?

_____

_____

_____

_____

_____

_____

_____

_____

_____

_____

_____

_____

_____

_____

_____

_____

_____

_____

Where were you?

_____

_____

_____

_____

_____

_____

_____

_____

_____

_____

_____

_____

_____

_____

_____

_____

_____

_____

_____

What did you attract in that state?

_____

_____

_____

_____

_____

_____

_____

_____

_____

_____

_____

_____

_____

_____

_____

_____

_____

_____

How did you feel?

_____

_____

_____

_____

_____

_____

_____

_____

_____

_____

_____

_____

_____

_____

_____

_____

_____

_____

"What we attract is a direct reflection of our energetic state"

CREATE A HIGH VIBE/LOW VIBE LIST

One of my favorite things to do when I need to realign my energy is to make a high vibe and low vibe list. Physically writing down the things that give me energy vs. the things that drain me helps me clearly see the action steps I need to take to feel good now.

You can make this experience extra special by choosing an ideal environment that supports you. For example, a few days ago, I decided to charge my energy by making my lists at a swanky cocktail bar in my neighborhood. I took a shower, spritzed myself with my favorite perfume, and chose an outfit I felt fabulous in. I brought my Louis Vuitton agenda and a gold pen rather than using my phone to jot down my thoughts. I ordered a glass of champagne and sat by candlelight as I made my lists. *The entire experience felt intentional and luxurious.*

Here is an example of my high vibe list:

- Wearing a white robe
- Listening to French jazz
- Getting a good night's sleep

It doesn't have to be a fancy cocktail bar and you don't have to use a designer agenda, but treating yourself to the best things you have access to makes all the difference in the world. The way you treat yourself sends a powerful message to the universe. You are worth every single thing you desire. You are worth the time, energy, and luxury you've told yourself you don't deserve. *It's time to change the conversation around what you are available for.*

MAKE A HIGH VIBE LIST

Write down all the things that make you feel energized. Some examples to get you started: indulging in self-care, getting into your zone of genius in your business, eating well, spending time with friends and family, being creative. This list is meant to remind you of and lead you to all things that feel good.

_____

_____

_____

_____

_____

_____

_____

_____

_____

_____

_____

_____

_____

_____

_____

MAKE A LOW VIBE LIST

Write down all the things that drain you. Some examples to get you started: comparing yourself to others, spending too much time online, invoicing clients, beating yourself up over past mistakes. This list is meant to remind you of and lead you *away* from all the things that *do not* feel good.

_____

_____

_____

_____

_____

_____

_____

_____

_____

_____

_____

_____

_____

_____

In order to do your best work, it is imperative you remain in a high vibration as often as possible. Energy is everything. You cannot create quality content from a low vibration.

Feeling good NOW is the single most important thing you can do for your business.

"You cannot create quality content from a low vibration"

ACTION STEPS FOR RAISING YOUR VIBRATION

The good news is that you can amp up your own vibe no matter what is going on around you. Here are some ideas:

Write your own powerful affirmations. Here's one I love: My natural vibration is of joy, clarity, energy, and love. I redirect any thoughts that do not serve my highest self.

Go for a workout or a walk. Exercise releases endorphins and boosts our mood. The quickest way to shift your energy is to change up your environment. Hit the gym or go for a power walk with your favorite playlist.

Get dolled up! Don't underestimate the power of glamour. When we look good, we feel good. And the way you present yourself as a business woman is crucial to your success. Think about it: would you want to hire someone who didn't care for themselves and appeared sloppy and lazy? It's time to step up your personal style.

It doesn't have to be expensive, but small enhancements to your appearance like making sure your clothing is clean and ironed, adding fun accessories, keeping your nails neatly manicured, and keeping up with your hair color can make you feel like a million bucks. And when you feel like a million bucks, well, you can guess what begins to happen.

Hydrate and eat well. Water is the most powerful way to flush out energetically-draining toxins from your body and help you feel energized. Research suggests drinking half your body weight in ounces to maintain balance in your body. There are also nutrient-rich foods that raise your vibration such as leafy greens, fresh fruits, beans, and anti-oxidant-rich teas. Avoid processed foods, as these can cloud you and make you feel lethargic and groggy. Remember: a healthy body means a healthy business.

Get outside and look at the sky. Realize that life is so much bigger than you are and opportunities are endless. One of my favorite things is to get lost in the clouds. It takes you out of your current reality and allows your thoughts to wander into a space of optimism and positivity.

Give back. Find a charity or organization to donate your time, money, or personal items to (clothes you may have cleaned out from your closet, furniture you may have planned to discard). Find a younger woman to mentor if you can. Get involved in women's events and offer to speak on a panel or at a meeting to share your experience.

Practice kindness. Call someone and offer them a loving word of encouragement. Smile at a stranger. Buy someone a coffee. Random acts of kindness hold an incredible amount of positive energy and can supercharge your vibe instantly.

Prioritize sleep. When we are well-rested, we think more clearly and have more energy. Be sure you are getting at least 7 hours of sleep per night. Stick to a bedtime routine that encourages you to go to bed around the same time every night. A consistent sleep schedule is key to success.

Choose items from the list above or create your own action steps for raising your vibration:

How will you raise your vibration?

_____

_____

_____

_____

_____

_____

_____

_____

_____

_____

_____

_____

_____

_____

_____

_____

How will you implement these experiences into your life?

_____

_____

_____

_____

_____

_____

_____

_____

_____

_____

_____

_____

_____

_____

_____

_____

_____

_____

_____

How will you implement these experiences into your business?

_____

_____

_____

_____

_____

_____

_____

_____

_____

_____

_____

_____

_____

_____

_____

_____

_____

_____

_____

What will you gain from raising your vibration?

_____

_____

_____

_____

_____

_____

_____

_____

_____

_____

_____

_____

_____

_____

_____

_____

_____

_____

How will your business change if you live in a higher vibe?

_____

_____

_____

_____

_____

_____

_____

_____

_____

_____

_____

_____

_____

_____

_____

_____

_____

_____

DAILY RITUAL:

CREATE YOUR ENERGETIC OUTLINE

Each morning, ask yourself: how can I raise my vibration today? An easy way to think about this is: what do I need more of in my life? What do I need less of in my life? And build your day around that answer.

THE WOMAN YOU WANT TO BE

"I didn't know what I wanted to do, but I always knew the woman I wanted to be."

- Diane Von Furstenburg

What if you could use every single instance where you are tempted to choose fear, scarcity, and insecurity and instead choose love, abundance, and confidence? — and I'm not talking about that fake cockiness, I'm talking a real sense of self-worth and a true knowing that you have so much to offer this world.

What if you could catch yourself in those moments where you're tempted to gossip, hate, panic, or envy, and instead, ask yourself: What would the BEST version of me do here? I believe self-development is a daily practice. A religion. Something we must continuously study and habitualize.

Evolved women are never done growing. They are aware that they are changing every moment of every day in every moment they find an opportunity to. They are obsessively choosing ways to love themselves, their lives, and others.

One of the most thrilling, creatively energizing, and empowering truths is that we get to choose the kind of business woman we want to be. Throughout my career, I have constantly examined myself, reinvented myself, and built myself into a woman I am incredibly proud of.

Before anyone does business with you, they will likely want to feel you out as a person. Can they trust you? Do they connect with you? Do they respect you? Are they inspired by you? Are they motivated by you? These are all questions potential clients and partners may ask themselves as they consider working with you.

The kind of woman you are will determine the kind of people you work with. In order to work with high-quality people, you must be sure you are a high-quality woman. Even if you've been in business for a while and achieved success, it's always helpful to revisit the vision for who you are. Where can you upgrade? What can you release?

Something as simple as your tone in an email can have a profound impact on the way people perceive you, and the way you feel about yourself.

WHAT KIND OF WOMAN DO YOU WANT TO BE?

In the space below, write down the kind of business woman you want to be:

_____

_____

_____

_____

_____

How can you fully embody this woman?

_____

_____

_____

_____

_____

_____

_____

_____

_____

_____

_____

_____

_____

_____

_____

_____

_____

What specific action steps will you take to be this woman?

_____

_____

_____

_____

_____

_____

_____

_____

_____

_____

_____

_____

_____

_____

_____

_____

_____

Does the way you are currently living align with this woman?

_____

_____

_____

_____

_____

_____

_____

_____

_____

_____

_____

_____

_____

_____

_____

_____

_____

Does the way you are currently thinking align with this woman?

_____

_____

_____

_____

_____

_____

_____

_____

_____

_____

_____

_____

_____

_____

_____

_____

_____

_____

In order to truly put that vision into action, we must first let our past selves go. It is time to release your past failures, mistakes, limiting beliefs, and anything that no longer serves your highest good.

Many women are afraid to evolve because others may judge them. "Who does she think she is?" I've heard that line a few times. Here me out ladies: It is safe to level up. You can remember where you came from, but never be afraid to evolve. Honor your roots while transforming into the best version of yourself.

In the space below, write down what you are letting go of:

_____

_____

_____

_____

_____

_____

_____

_____

_____

_____

_____

_____

"Your ideal self is completely attainable. Becoming a successful business woman is possible for everyone. You have the power to achieve all of your goals, create the energetic boundaries required for your success, and command respect from your clients and peers. Nobody is responsible for crowning you. You must anoint yourself a high-end woman."

Write down the core values you want to cultivate as a powerful woman in business:

_____

_____

_____

_____

_____

_____

_____

_____

_____

_____

_____

_____

_____

_____

_____

_____

_____

_____

What strengths do you currently possess?

_____

_____

_____

_____

_____

_____

_____

_____

_____

_____

_____

_____

_____

_____

_____

_____

_____

Write down the areas you'd like to improve upon:

_____

_____

_____

_____

_____

_____

_____

_____

_____

_____

_____

_____

_____

_____

_____

_____

_____

How can you work on those areas that need improvement in the next 7 days?

_____

_____

_____

_____

_____

_____

_____

_____

_____

_____

_____

_____

_____

_____

How can you work on those areas that need improvement in the next 30 days?

_____

_____

_____

_____

_____

_____

_____

_____

_____

_____

_____

_____

_____

_____

_____

_____

_____

_____

ESTABLISHING YOUR WORTH

When it comes to business, much like in life, you set the tone for how you are treated. If you are attracting clients who want everything for free, there is likely something about your energy that is making them feel comfortable to ask for everything for free!

On the other hand, if clients are willing to pay top-dollar for your products and services, it is likely that you created that vibe through establishing trust, producing quality work, and emitting an energy of self-worth.

So how exactly do you emit that energy?

Here are some ways you can establish yourself as someone who is highly sought after, respected, and paid well:

Create boundaries. There is a fine line between being approachable and being abused. Your time is precious. Think about where you are spending most of your energy. If you're answering emails and Facebook messages all day from people who have not yet hired you, you are wearing yourself thin. Can you create an FAQ page with common questions on your website? Create an auto-responder email with those common questions? This allows you to come from a place of service, but do it on a massive scale. You get to help people, but protect your energy. It's truly a win/win.

Be unapologetic. Be who you are, all the time. There's no reason to hide your true self. Your ideal clients and partners will find you when you're authentically expressing yourself without apology. If you're attracting clients by being too generic or imitating someone else, that just won't be sustainable in the long-run. Being your true self requires a thick skin, but once you get into your flow and start working with people who love you for you, you will be unstoppable. As Dita Von Teese said, "You can be the ripest, juiciest peach in the world, and there's still going to be somebody who hates peaches." Successful women are not afraid of being disliked.

"Successful women are not afraid of being disliked."

Exude professionalism. Be sure that your website, social media, personal style, and attitude are all professional. This does not mean you have to be boring! Some of the most authentic and creative women are incredibly professional and poised. You can have pink hair and have the respect of the masses. You can speak your truth and make millions of dollars. Being professional is about respecting yourself and those around you. It's about taking the high road, eliminating drama from your world, and remaining focused on your work.

Create quality work. When it comes to creating content for public consumption, value is the most important thing to keep in mind. Whether it's a podcast, a blog, or a Facebook post, think about every single piece of content you're putting out into the world. Your public content is like the appetizer before a beautiful main course. You're giving potential clients a delicious taste of what's to come. Why are people visiting your space? Are they coming to be inspired? Entertained? Informed? Be sure you're giving them that. Leave the drama at home and focus on adding value constantly. When it comes to paid work, remember that your clients are your business card. If your client has a stellar experience with you, they're going to talk about it. They're going to come back to you for more. On the other hand, if they have a negative experience, they're going to shout it from the roof tops. Your credibility is the most important thing in business. Your reputation takes years to build and seconds to become tarnished. Even when clients are challenging, always take the high road and choose to be professional.

What boundaries do you have in your business?

_____

_____

_____

_____

_____

_____

_____

If you have none, which need to be established?

_____

_____

_____

_____

_____

_____

_____

_____

Are you truly being yourself, unapologetically?

_____

_____

_____

_____

_____

_____

_____

_____

If not, how can you be more yourself?

_____

_____

_____

_____

_____

_____

_____

_____

How do you exude professionalism?

_____

_____

_____

_____

_____

_____

_____

Which areas of your business need to be more professional?

_____

_____

_____

_____

_____

_____

_____

_____

Is the quality of your public content up to a high standard?

_____

_____

_____

_____

_____

_____

_____

_____

How can you increase the value of your public content?

_____

_____

_____

_____

_____

_____

_____

_____

_____

Are you providing exceptional experiences for your clients?

_____

_____

_____

_____

_____

_____

_____

What areas of your work can be improved?

_____

_____

_____

_____

_____

_____

_____

_____

"A woman becomes a force once she knows what she wants and learns how to ask for it."

THE POWER OF THE PERSONAL UPGRADE

Something incredible clicks when we decide to upgrade our lives. Whether it's moving into a new home or something as simple as refreshing your wardrobe, there is power in your personal upgrade.

When you invite better things into your life, you immediately shift. Everything feels elevated. Abundance begins to flow to you. The way you treat yourself is a conversation with the universe.

What areas of your life can be upgraded? (ex: Do you need a few new key wardrobe staples? Do you need to refresh your makeup? Does your home need to be redecorated to support your success?)

_____

_____

_____

_____

_____

_____

_____

_____

_____

_____

_____

What areas of your business can be upgraded? (ex: Do you need a professional photo shoot? A new website?)

_____

_____

_____

_____

_____

_____

_____

_____

_____

_____

Do you struggle with guilt around upgrading your life?

_____

_____

_____

_____

_____

_____

_____

_____

If so, where does that guilt come from?

_____

_____

_____

_____

_____

_____

_____

_____

How does guilt serve you?

_____

_____

_____

_____

_____

_____

_____

How can you commit to putting yourself first?

_____

_____

_____

_____

_____

_____

_____

_____

How can you commit to upgrading your business?

_____

_____

_____

_____

_____

_____

_____

_____

_____

Here's the thing many female entrepreneurs have yet to understand: the quality of your life is your business card.

The more you love yourself and your life, the more you will attract your ideal clients. When you are obsessed with your own way of living, you will become irresistible to your dream audience. People will be drawn to you.

The trick is actually creating that life, in big or small ways – not faking it. So many women are running businesses that preach the importance of treating yourself well, upleveling your life, and investing in yourself – but they are doing none of that.

Answer the following questions honestly:

Are you being true to your brand?

_____

_____

_____

_____

_____

_____

_____

Do you feel qualified to teach/sell/serve whatever you are promoting?

_____

_____

_____

_____

_____

_____

_____

How can you align with your message?

_____

_____

_____

_____

_____

_____

_____

_____

What do you have to gain by living your truth?

_____

_____

_____

_____

_____

_____

_____

_____

DAILY RITUAL:

CREATE YOURSELF

Each morning, upon waking up, ask yourself: How do I want to show up in the world today? Who do I want to be? How can I be her?

BE A VISIONISTA

Without a clear vision of how you want your business to look and feel, it's impossible to stay focused and achieve success. Some of the most successful people in the world, especially professional athletes, use this form of mental preparation to achieve their most high-reaching goals.

Going through an imagery practice allows you to feel as if you've already had the experience you wish to have. It sets your mind up to think it's already happened, so that when the time actually comes, you feel more prepared. Using visualization to imagine yourself in the most favorable circumstances is one of the biggest tools for success.

Emily Cook, of the U.S. freestyle ski team, uses imagery as mental training for the Olympics. She believes in engaging all senses when preparing for her aerial jumps. "You have to smell it. You have to hear it. You have to feel it, everything," she said in a New York Times article. Cook even imagines and then records herself reading a detailed script including what she sees, hears, and feels in her mind, and then plays that recording back with her eyes closed in a relaxed state. She literally creates her own, custom meditation.

Other high-functioning people who have used visualization techniques to activate their success are Jim Carrey, Oprah Winfrey, Will Smith, and professional skier and gold medalist Lindsey Vonn. Jim Carrey shared his own experiences on the Oprah Winfrey show around how visualization has affected his career. He told Oprah, "I used to park my car in the Mulholland drive, LA every night, and I would visualize seeing myself that directors are interested in me, the people that I respected, saying that, they like my work. I would visualize that things are coming to me. I had nothing at that time, but it just made me feel better. I would drive home and think that I do have these things. I also wrote a check for myself for 10 million dollars for the acting services rendered, kept in my wallet, and I gave myself three years to manifest. I dated it 1995 Thanksgiving. To my surprise, just before the Thanksgiving 1994, I found that I am going to get 10 million dollars for the movie Dumb and Dumber."

QUESTIONS TO HELP YOU VISUALIZE YOUR SUCCESS

What do you want in your business? Where do you imagine yourself working from every day? Where do you live? Are you in a luxurious penthouse apartment in New York City, listening to jazz while you brew your steaming-hot espresso every morning? Are you on a remote beach in Bali, hearing the waves crash as you indulge in a fresh fruit bowl while answering your emails? Do you picture yourself sitting in a luxe hotel lobby, sipping on an ice-cold glass of champagne while you take a call from your editor about your next book? Are you sitting first class on a flight to Los Angeles, heading to meet your VIP client at the Beverly Hills Hotel? Do you have on a brand-new pair of nude Christian Louboutin pumps? Do you smell like Chanel No. 5? Are you taking morning SoulCycle classes to jump start your day?

It's important to get lost in a *multisensory experience* when using visualization techniques. Allow yourself to get creative, feel the sensations in your body, and dream without limitations.

CREATE A MULTISENSORY VISUALIZATION RITUAL

Think about something you'd love to happen in your business. Close your eyes, and begin to imagine it happening in great detail. Be sure to engage all five senses. Spend as long as you like in this space, really allowing yourself to see it all unfolding as you want it to.

Take it a step further and record your visualization into your phone so you can use it as a form of guided meditation any time you need a boost!

ITS ALL IN YOUR HEAD

Visualization may be more powerful than you realize. There's a fascinating study on brain patters in weightlifters. It found that the patterns activated in a weightlifter's brain when lifting hundreds of pounds were similarly activated when they only imagined lifting those weights.

Guang Yue, an exercise psychologist from Cleveland Clinic Foundation in Ohio, compared "people who went to the gym with people who carried out virtual workouts in their heads". He discovered a 30% muscle increase in the group who went to the gym. But get this - the group of participants who conducted mental exercises of the weight training increased muscle strength by 13.5% - almost half as much. This average remained for 3 months following the mental training. That goes to show you the power of our minds. This data was found in Psychology Today, and you can read up on more of it on your own if you're interested.

"Your thoughts create your reality. Make sure they are fabulous."

LIMITLESS LUXE MEDITATION PRACTICE

The most important thing to understand is that we have the power to imagine positive things happening right now. Even if you aren't yet bringing in the revenue you desire, or your client list is lacking, you must imagine it happening first, before the universe matches that desire. You must get into the vibration of having it before it actually happens.

If you read my book *Girl Code: Unlocking the Secrets to Success, Sanity, and Happiness for the Female Entrepreneur*, then you're familiar with the idea of Limitless Luxe. Use your imagination to visualize exactly how you want your business to look and feel. Start by spending 5 minutes per day in meditation picturing everything you aspire to have in your career. Repeat your Limitless Luxe meditation daily, working up to 10 or 15 minutes per day, and pay attention to the changes you start to notice.

When you detach from an outcome, you take your power back.

VISUALIZING VS. CLINGING

It's important to note that visualizing success is different from clinging to a specific outcome. It can be challenging for a driven, ambitious woman to understand that she cannot control a situation, and she certainly cannot predict the way something may unfold.

Life happens in mysterious ways, and often times we are presented with something even better than we could have imagined. Show up, work hard, but also let the universe work its magic.

Spend time visualizing what you want, but also practice detachment. Know that what is for you will never pass you, and you always get what you need. That's how you take your power back. That's how you experience true success.

THE POWER OF AFFIRMATIONS

Along with visualization, powerful affirmations can also supercharge our success. Affirmations were developed in the 1970's by neuroscientists, and they are meant to incorporate psychotherapy and linguistics in order to consciously rewire thought patterns towards more desired outcomes. In other words, affirmations are power phrases that help us think more positively and ultimately achieve our goals.

22 AFFIRMATIONS FOR SUCCESS

- I am a magnet for wealth and abundance
- I attract my dream clients with ease
- I am infinitely powerful
- I intuitively know my next steps
- I run my business with pride, clarity, and ease
- I am a high-end woman
- Ideas and creativity flow to me easily
- My business is effortlessly successful
- I am focused, fearless, and free
- My energy is limitless
- I am a force
- Success is my birthright
- I am highly valued and sought after by quality clients
- I am a perfect vibrational match for my dreams
- I am filled with gratitude for my business
- I am calm and solution-oriented
- My business is a luxury brand
- I am capable of every dream and worthy of every desire
- I am only available for thoughts of magic
- I naturally attract everything I need to be successful
- I believe in myself and my business
- I am an endless resource of money-making ideas

Here are the ideal times to practice your affirmations. The more you read them and/or say them out loud, the more powerful they become:

Upon waking up. Your mind is fresh, rested, and open to new ideas. Set the tone for your day by carefully choosing your words.

Whenever you feel stressed. The perfect antidote to stress is a positive thought. Clear out the negative clutter in your mind by repeating one of your power phrases and feel your energy shift immediately.

Before a client meeting, speaking engagement, or networking event. Use your affirmations as a reset button for your mind. Get into a positive headspace before presenting yourself to others.

DAILY RITUAL:

DESIGN YOUR OWN AFFIRMATIONS

In the space below, write your own affirmations. You can use the list above to inspire you, or create your own custom ones that suit your goals.

_____

_____

_____

_____

_____

_____

_____

_____

_____

_____

_____

_____

CURATING YOUR CIRCLE

Getting in the right mindset for success requires a deep and honest look at who you are spending your time with. You don't necessarily need to be surrounded by other entrepreneurs, but you do need to be surrounded by quality people in order to stay focused, positive, and feel supported.

Answer the following questions honestly:

Who are you spending the majority of your time with?

_____

_____

_____

_____

_____

Who is the first person you speak to in the morning?

_____

_____

_____

_____

_____

Who are you texting all day?

_____

_____

_____

_____

Who are you having dinner with most nights?

_____

_____

_____

_____

Who do you chat with over cocktails?

_____

_____

_____

_____

Who do you share business wins with?

_____

_____

_____

_____

Who do you tell your new ideas to?

_____

_____

_____

_____

Who do you go to for advice?

_____

_____

_____

_____

Who do you share frustrations/challenges with?

_____

_____

_____

_____

Take a good, hard look at your answers and ask yourself: do these people enhance my life and support my journey to success?

If the answer is yes, that's fabulous! Be sure to spend as much time with those people as possible. And, check in with yourself to be sure you are reciprocating that good energy.

If the answer is no, it's time to make some changes. Rather than thinking about cutting everyone out immediately, think about adding new and inspiring people into your world.

Here are a few ways to meet like-minded people:

Check out MeetUp.com and search for groups in your area that will inspire you. For example, "Lady Bosses of Austin, TX" or "Women in Tech in the Hudson Valley." Not only will you find like-minded people in your area, you will have the opportunity to meet them in person (how retro!) Don't see one in your area? Create it!

Find Facebook groups with like-minded women. For example, my group, The Slay Baby Collective, has over 12,000 supportive, inspiring women interested in creating genuine friendships. I've had the pleasure of watching relationships bloom both on and offline through that group. Seek out groups that are focused on positivity and any interests that you may have.

The people you spend your time with will determine the quality of your conversations, your thoughts, and ultimately your world.

THINGS TO KEEP IN MIND WHEN CURATING YOUR CIRCLE

Spend your time with people who are focused on success, self-worth, and happiness

Spend your time with people who would rather talk about goals than gossip

Spend your time with people who are more interested in moving forward rather than looking back

Spend your time with people who want to see you win

CURATING YOUR SOCIAL MEDIA

A study by Deloitte found that Americans collectively check their smart phones more than 8 billion times per day.

On average, people in the U.S. check their smart phones more than 46 times per day. Sound alarming? I know.

And most people said they look at their mobile device within five minutes of waking up.

Think about that: every single time you open your phone and load an app, specifically social media, you are consuming information that will have some sort of an impact on you. If you load Instagram before you've had your morning coffee, and you find yourself looking at someone else's vacation photos, how do you think that will affect your day? Will it help you make money, create killer content, or attract your dream clients? Probably not.

Clearly, our virtual realities are just as important as our actual realities. The average person spends two hours per day on social media (which converts to 5 years and 4 months over the course of a lifetime). And if you're working your business online, that number is much higher.

QUESTIONS TO HELP YOU CURATE YOUR ONLINE FEEDS

How does social media inspire you?

_____

_____

_____

_____

_____

_____

How does social media drain you?

_____

_____

_____

_____

_____

_____

_____

_____

Who are you following right now that brings you energy?

_____

_____

_____

_____

_____

_____

_____

Who are you following right now that drains you?

_____

_____

_____

_____

_____

_____

_____

Who are you following right now that makes you feel envious?

_____

_____

_____

_____

_____

_____

_____

Is it possible for you to shift that envy into inspiration?

_____

_____

_____

_____

_____

_____

_____

Do you pick up your phone within 5 minutes of waking up?

_____

_____

_____

_____

_____

_____

_____

How does that make you feel?

_____

_____

_____

_____

_____

_____

_____

How much time are you spending online per day?

_____

_____

_____

_____

_____

_____

_____

Are you comfortable with that number?

_____

_____

_____

_____

_____

_____

_____

Do you feel you need a social media detox?

_____

_____

_____

_____

_____

_____

_____

If yes, how will you implement that into your life?

_____

_____

_____

_____

_____

_____

_____

How will a social media detox empower you?

_____

_____

_____

_____

_____

_____

_____

_____

_____

_____

_____

_____

_____

_____

_____

_____

_____

_____

_____

DAILY RITUAL:

CURATION STATION

What "channel" are you tuning into each day? Who are you talking to most? What are you watching online? Remember: you are in charge of what you are consuming. Make changes as necessary!

WHAT TO DO WHEN YOU FEEL STUCK

I've never met a business woman who hasn't felt stuck at some point in her career. Funks are a part of the process. It's normal to feel confused, lost, or uninspired in our work. And it can happen for many reasons: perhaps you are exhausted, burnt out, bored, spending too much time comparing yourselves to others, or you simply need a break!

No matter the reason, the worst thing you can do when you feel blocked is worry about feeling blocked. The more stress we add to a situation, the worse we feel, and the longer it takes us to become unstuck.

Remember: you can choose the woman you want to be! Do you want to be the woman who remains consumed by stress and fear? Or do you want to be the woman who is solution-oriented, positive, and focused on her goals?

WHY YOU MAY FEEL STUCK AND HOW TO GET UNSTUCK

You're lacking confidence. It's time to get real with yourself. Is there a new skill you need to learn to stay ahead in your industry? Do your current skills need sharpening? Find the root of the issue and address it.

You're ignoring your intuition. It's important to lean on others in business and have a strong support system, but if we're asking too many people for their opinion, we can lose sight of our own vision. Take yourself out on a solo date and journal about what you truly want – not what you "should" want, or what you think you are supposed to be doing. What do you want for your business? What does success look like to you?

You're spending too much time in your head. Overthinking kills our creativity and motivation. If you feel like you're spinning your wheels, it's time to get into action. Set one small goal for your business and get out there and make it happen. You'll build confidence and momentum, and when you're in action mode, you don't have time to obsess over anything but success!

You're choosing thoughts that scare you. We create stories in our minds constantly. Are you telling yourself stories about failure or about success?

You're comparing yourself to everyone around you. We all know that comparison is the thief of joy. The energy spent stalking other business women on Instagram could be energy spent creating beautiful things, making a ton of money, or enjoying your well-deserved freedom that comes along with success.

You haven't reinvented yourself in a while. There is nothing like a good business or lifestyle makeover to jolt us into action. Everything gets tired after a while; our wardrobe, our home office décor, our website, our logo. If you're feeling stuck, take it as a cue to survey your surroundings and think about what needs updating.

You're focusing on what's lacking. Gratitude is the practice of shifting the focus from what's missing to what we have. Pour your energy into being grateful for everything you have. As Oprah says, "I live in the space of thankfulness — and for that, I have been rewarded a million times over. I started out giving thanks for small things, and the more thankful I became, the more my bounty increased. That's because — for sure — what you focus on expands. When you focus on the goodness in life, you create more of it."

In the space below, journal about an area of your business you feel blocked in:

_____

_____

_____

_____

_____

_____

_____

_____

What does your intuition tell you about this block?

_____

_____

_____

_____

_____

_____

_____

_____

What can you be doing less of to help move you closer to your goals?

_____

_____

_____

_____

_____

_____

_____

What action steps are you going to take right now to get unstuck?

_____

_____

_____

_____

_____

_____

_____

Who would you be if you took those action steps?

_____

_____

_____

_____

_____

_____

_____

_____

MANTRAS FOR GETTING IN MOTION

It is safe for me to move forward with fresh energy

I am willing to leave my past behind me

I have everything I need to succeed right now

I am creative and filled with positive momentum

It is safe for me to show up as the most authentic version of myself

I am grateful for what I have, and excited for what's to come

I am no longer available for jealousy

I am ready for abundance and worthy of success

DAILY RITUAL:

GETTING INTO ACTION

Identify any areas you may feel blocked. Determine 1 action step you can take today to help you get in motion.

HABITS OF HIGHLY SUCCESSFUL WOMEN

There are many common threads between successful, professional women. Some swear by waking up at 4:00 am, while others can't live without their nightly bubble bath. Some need to work out daily, while others prefer to listen to their bodies and only exercise if they feel energized.

The main thing all successful women have in common is that they are intentional about their time.

When is the last time you truly feel like you owned your day? Below are some suggestions on how to reclaim your time and implement routines and success rituals that support your best self. Try incorporating some of these into your week, or create your own.

QUESTIONS TO ASK YOURSELF UPON WAKING UP

What is my intention for the day?

What are my top 3 priorities for the day?

What am I grateful for today?

What happened yesterday that did not serve me? What can I eliminate from today?

MORNING RITUALS FOR SUCCESS

Your morning routine can completely transform your mindset. No matter how busy you are, it's important to know you can create pockets of time for yourself. Even 15 minutes can have a profound impact on the way you think and feel. Here are some suggestions for rituals to incorporate into your morning.

Gratitude: List 5 things you're thankful for before you get out of bed

Creative exploration: Search Pinterest for inspiring imagery, flip through your favorite magazine for some great articles, read or watch interviews with inspirational women

Wipe down your desk and organize your paperwork

Use your intuition to direct your next step: Does your body feel like working out that day? Are you tired? Do you need more sleep? Do you need a personal day?

Take an energizing bubble bath with essential oils

Go for a 15-minute power walk in the fresh air

QUESTIONS TO ASK YOURSELF BEFORE GOING TO BED

How do I feel about today?

Did I achieve what I set out to?

What am I grateful for tonight?

What can I release?

EVENING RITUALS FOR SUCCESS

Take a detox bubble bath with Epsom salts and essential oils

Write a "celebration" list of everything you accomplished that day (think of this as the opposite of a "to-do" list)

Tidy up and take care of household chores so your home feels fresh in the morning

Set your intention for the next day

Send love to any issue/challenge that is frustrating you and release it

Do a mini meditation (10 minutes or less)

THE POWER OF THE WHITE ROBE

Often times, the smallest, most inexpensive changes have the biggest impact on the way we feel. I always talk about the "power" of my white bath robe. I sometimes spend an entire morning in mine, drinking coffee, working, or just lounging (something that is admittedly hard for me to do). Fluffy, floor length white robes make me feel like I'm living in a five-star hotel - one of my ultimate fantasies. They represent luxury and comfort. I take a bath, spritz on perfume, and sometimes even put on a piece of jewelry with it. When I'm wearing my robe, I feel powerful and glamorous. This directly impacts the content I create, and the way I show up in my business.

Think about some small upgrades you can make in your own life that help you feel more successful. What changes can help you raise your vibe so that you can focus on your goals and feel unstoppable?

RITUAL AND ROUTINE CHECK-IN

How do you feel about your morning and evening routines?

_____

_____

_____

_____

_____

_____

_____

_____

What are some new rituals you will commit to introducing into your life?

_____

_____

_____

_____

_____

_____

_____

_____

_____

_____

_____

_____

_____

_____

_____

_____

_____

Successful women may design their days differently, but there are a few things they all do similarly – and that's the way they think. There are certain perspectives, thoughts, and values that contribute to a success mindset, and I've listed a few for you below.

10 THINGS WOMEN WHO VALUE THEMSELVES DO DIFFERENTLY:

They confidently ask for what they want

They listen to their gut + trust themselves

They don't seek the approval of others

They don't make decision in a low vibration

They don't do things out of desperation

They move forward even if nobody understands their vision

They do not make excuses for themselves or anyone else

They don't allow their past to define their future

They don't put their happiness in the hands of someone else

They don't determine their success based on external wins or accomplishments

DAILY RITUAL:

BE INTENTIONAL WITH YOUR TIME

Remember that your time is valuable! Be intentional with it. Think about where you can create pockets of time to help you focus in on your goals, raise your vibration, and set yourself up for success.

STEP INTO YOUR POWER

Truly standing in your power is the ultimate key to success. You can have all the knowledge, experience, and tools to hit your goals, but if you do not feel powerful, it's all worthless.

In this module, I'm going to share the best ways you can fully step into your power and rid yourself of the distractions that may hold you back in your business.

RELEASING PAST FAILURES

A strong success-mindset requires letting go of past mistakes and failures. It requires self-forgiveness and completely reframing the way we view those mistakes and failures.

When is the last time you truly screwed up in business? Perhaps you flubbed a presentation in front of a room full of people. Maybe you overpromised a client and couldn't deliver and wound up losing a sale.

Whatever is was, I can bet you're still beating yourself up over it. It's time to let it go! It's time to understand that we are all human, and every single "failure" is a learning experience. If we never fail, we never grow, and stagnant women don't change the world.

In the space below, journal about a time you believe you failed

_____

_____

_____

_____

_____

_____

_____

_____

_____

_____

_____

_____

_____

_____

_____

_____

_____

What can you learn from that failure?

_____

_____

_____

_____

_____

_____

_____

_____

_____

_____

_____

_____

_____

_____

_____

_____

_____

How would life change if you viewed that failure as an opportunity to grow?

_____

_____

_____

_____

_____

_____

_____

_____

_____

_____

_____

_____

_____

_____

_____

_____

_____

How would life change if you forgave yourself?

_____

_____

_____

_____

_____

_____

_____

_____

_____

_____

_____

_____

_____

_____

_____

_____

_____

_____

_____

Write a mantra about releasing your past:

_____

_____

_____

_____

_____

_____

_____

_____

_____

_____

_____

_____

_____

_____

_____

_____

_____

_____

TRANSPARENCY WILL GET YOU EVERYWHERE

I'm going to let you in on a secret: the best way to overcome insecurity in your business is to be transparent. To practice vulnerability, and to own every single part of yourself. If you just shuddered, I get it. It's painfully challenging for most women to bare it all and truly share themselves with the world. But when you master this, you open up a world of power, abundance, and pure magic.

Your truth is your superpower. Your ability to connect with your ideal audience lies in your ability to be fully and completely yourself.

Now here's the kicker – sharing your truth requires a thick skin. Not everyone will understand you, but frankly, that's not your problem. You may lose a few followers, or ruffle a few feathers, but the integrity you will gain is worth its weight in gold.

I have personally struggled with this in my business. The larger my reach became, the more eyes I had on me. It became more of a challenge to unapologetically share things, because I risked people disliking me, and worse - expressing that dislike in a public forum.

But I got over it. And it's time for you to, as well. Here's how I did it. I simply made a list of everything that happened when I chose to be as authentic as possible.

Things that happen when I speak my truth:

I feel incredibly empowered

I feel confident

I feel energized

I feel inspired

I feel unstoppable

I gain followers

I lose followers

There is only one "negative" on that list, and I'm using quotes because truthfully, I don't want anyone following me who isn't fired up about what I have to say.

Stop asking yourself "Will they like me?" and start asking yourself "Do I like me?"

If you are 100% aligned with yourself, then the algorithms, followers, likes, gossip, unfollowers - none of it matters.

I believe in your honesty! You should too.

"Your confidence will make some people uncomfortable. Those are not your people."

What is one truth you have been afraid to share?

_____

_____

_____

_____

_____

_____

How would your business change if you could be 100% transparent?

_____

_____

_____

_____

_____

_____

How do you feel when you practice authenticity in your business?

_____

_____

_____

_____

_____

_____

_____

_____

_____

_____

_____

_____

_____

_____

_____

_____

_____

REDEFINING SUCCESS

Think about what success currently looks and feels like to you. Standing in your power means redefining success – on your own terms. Cultivating a mindset for success is not about doing what everyone else is doing. It's not about doing what your parents think you should do. It's about doing what feels good to you – now.

What does your current definition of success look like?

_____

_____

_____

_____

_____

_____

_____

_____

_____

_____

_____

_____

_____

Where did that definition come from?

_____

_____

_____

_____

_____

_____

_____

Do you currently feel successful?

_____

_____

_____

_____

_____

_____

_____

_____

How would you like to redefine success?

_____

_____

_____

_____

_____

_____

_____

How would your business change if you lived by your own definition of success?

_____

_____

_____

_____

_____

_____

_____

_____

DAILY RITUAL:

RISING UP

Practicing authenticity is a daily practice. Ask yourself every day: how can I rise up and show up in the world as the most powerful version of myself?

NOTES & REVELATIONS

Congratulations! You have given yourself a gift by completing this experience. Use the space below to reflect on the work you've done, document any revelations, and make any notes you wish. Remember, you can come back to this workbook at any time and update your answers as you evolve into your next level! These tools are yours forever.

_____

_____

_____

_____

_____

_____

_____

_____

_____

_____

_____

CONNECT WITH CARA

Learn more about Cara at www.CaraAlwill.com

Follow Cara on Instagram @TheChampagneDiet

Listen to Cara's podcast, Style Your Mind, on iTunes

Get Cara's other books including *Girl Code*, *Like She Owns The Place*, and the original *Style Your Mind* workbook on Amazon

ABOUT CARA

Cara Alwill Leyba is a best selling author and master life coach who encourages women to live their most effervescent lives, celebrate themselves every day, and make their happiness a priority. Over 4 million listeners worldwide tune in to her podcast Style Your Mind each week for powerful conversations and a mega dose of inspiration.

Cara's stylish and edgy approach to self-help has attracted thousands of women to attend her workshops and events around the country. She has been featured in *Glamour, Shape, Entrepreneur.com, Success, Cosmo, Marie Claire*, and many others.

As a social influencer, Cara reaches her following of over 100,000 fans across all her social media platforms and inspires them daily with lifestyle tips, mindset advice, business strategies, and does it all with a chic and fashionable flair. Cara has collaborated with Macy's, Kate Spade, SoulCycle, and others.